Porthminster Beach Café

The Cookbook

Editor: Joel Todd
Recipes: Michael Smith
Art direction: Peter Leung
Photography: Claudia Sanchiz Garin
Illustration: Mark Foreman
Sub editor: Kendra Futcher
Home economists: Anna Jones & Emily Ezekiel

First published 2013 by Porthminster Beach Café.

Printed at Pureprint Group on UPM Fine offset,
using vegetable inks throughout.
ISO 14001. FSC® certified and CarbonNeutral®.

ISBN 978-0-9576261-0-2

MIX
Paper from
responsible sources
FSC® C022913

Contents

Foreword

Picture an expanse of sandy beach, bright blue sea, warm sunshine and a light quality that is unique to this place. On the edge of this beach stands Porthminster Beach Café, a haven for foodies of all ages and a backdrop to good times.

Michael Smith, an Aussie by birth, has created a fantastic, relaxed dining experience that marries the best of Antipodean food culture with a celebration of Cornwall's amazing food produce. Frequently borrowing from the cooking of Asia and the Mediterranean, Michael has developed a unique style of cooking that is both modern and exciting.

This book is an opportunity to share a few of the dishes you'll find on the Café's menu. Personal favourites of mine include the much-loved Monkfish Curry, Seabass with Crab Fritters and Cornish Sardines with Red Onion, Rosemary and Lemon.

But, this book offers more than just recipes, with stories and images that truly capture the character and beauty of this part of Cornwall. It will definitely make you smile and hopefully encourage you to share the wonderful dishes created at Porthminster Beach Café with friends and family. Enjoy!

Nathan Outlaw, 2013

Introduction

Once a place purely for pasties and summertime fish and chips, Cornwall has evolved over the last two decades to become a year-round destination for food lovers, keen to experience the plentiful local produce first hand. St.Ives in particular is central to Cornwall's gastronomic revolution and is home to a diverse range of great places to eat, from delis to more refined dining. Porthminster Beach Café has been at the forefront of this transformation.

Perched at the top of the beach, the iconic white Art Deco building could not be more perfectly positioned to capture the picture-postcard views across St.Ives Bay and towards the harbour. And whilst the Cornish sun might not always shine as the postcards (or indeed this book) suggest, there really is no better place for lunch or dinner – inside or out. The Café isn't just close to the beach, it's part of it.

The food expresses a similar affinity with its locality, from the freshest of locally caught seafood, to vegetables and herbs grown in the Café's hillside garden. Australian-born chef Michael Smith brings a sense of imagination and adventure to the kitchen, using both Asian and Mediterranean flavours to great effect.

From simple lunchtime sardines to more sophisticated evening dishes, the recipes in this book convey the breadth and balance of the food created at Porthminster Beach Café. Long-term favourites such as Cornish Crab and Mussel Linguine are included alongside more unusual dishes such as Cider Braised Pork Cheeks.

This book is also a celebration of the Café's coming of age, marking its 21st year.

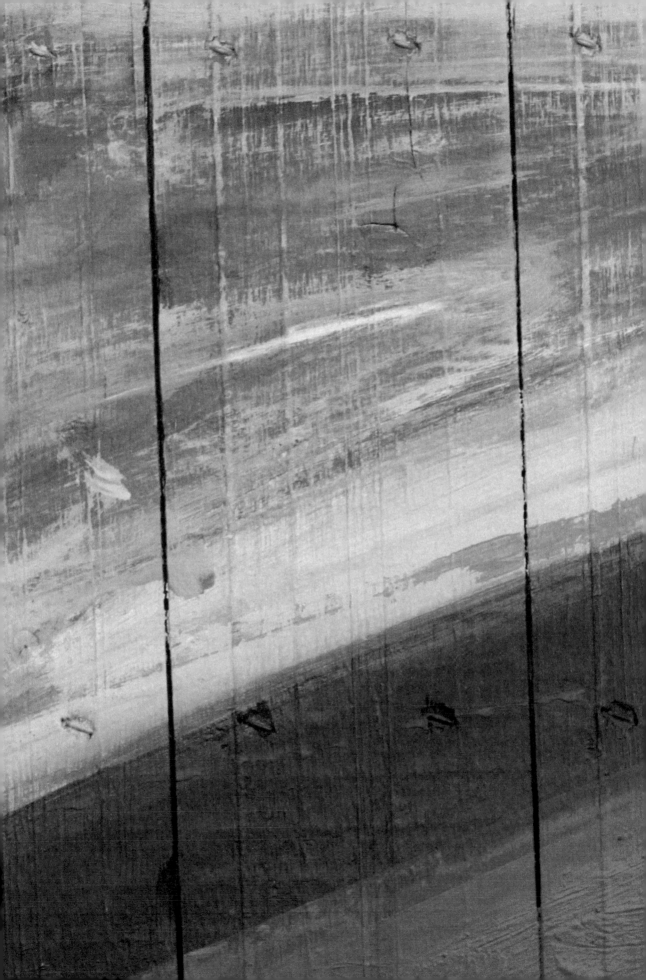

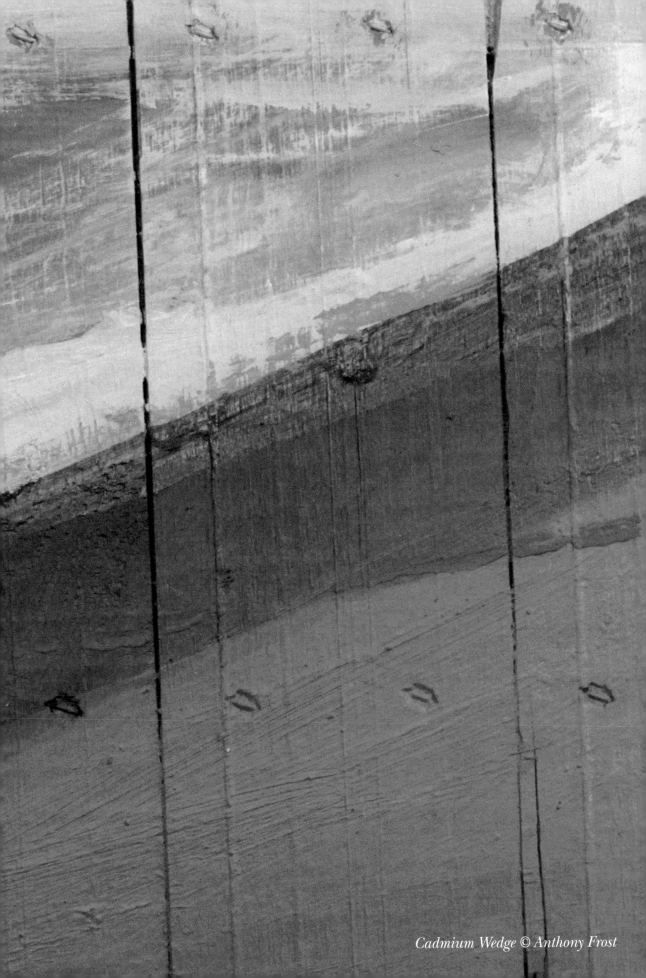

Cadmium Wedge © Anthony Frost

SEA

The sheer variety of fish and seafood found in Cornwall is astonishing - at certain times of year between 30 and 50 different types of species can be landed at Newlyn Market.

This diversity allows us to vary our cooking techniques, keeping the menu fresh and exciting.

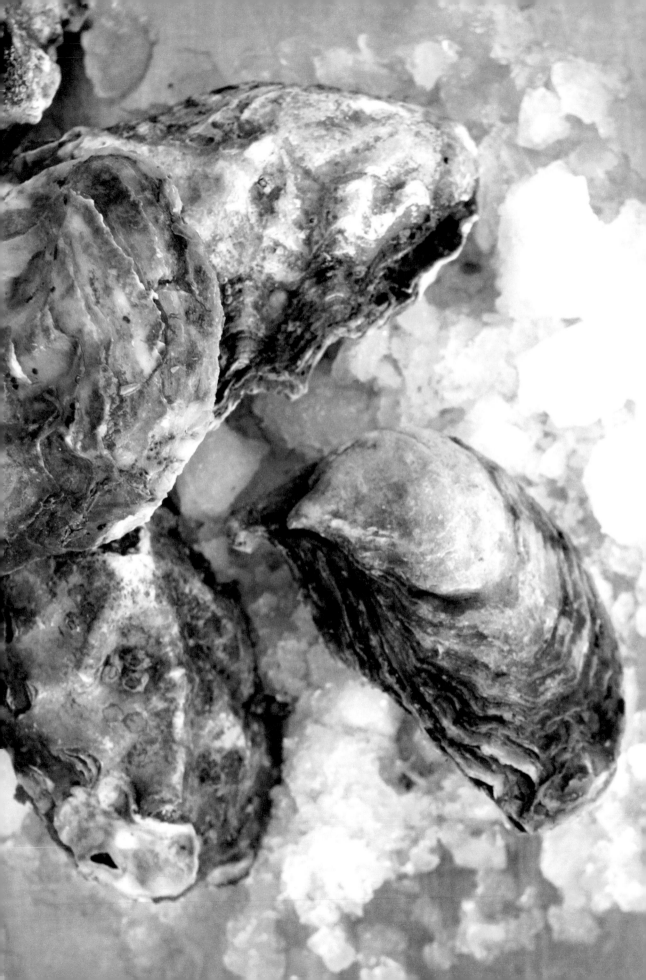

GRILLED OYSTERS
with Wasabi Mayonnaise
& Spicy Chorizo

When you're by the sea it's hard to beat the simplicity and freshness of a natural oyster with lemon or vinegar, but for variation try these cooked versions. Somehow the chorizo and wasabi work really well with the oysters' sea-salty freshness.

Serves 4

– 8 x fresh oysters, cleaned and opened
– 1 tsp of wasabi
– 2 egg yolks
– 2 tsp yuzu juice (or lime juice)
– 200ml vegetable oil
– 100g cooking chorizo, sliced
– Small bunch of coriander

Place the egg yolks, wasabi and yuzu together in a bowl. Whisk whilst slowly pouring in the oil until all the oil has been used. Add a little warm water if it becomes too thick.

Preheat the grill to high.

Lay the oysters on a baking tray, spoon enough mayonnaise to cover the oysters lightly, about half a teaspoon for each. Put a slice of chorizo on top and place under the grill for about 3 minutes or until golden. Sprinkle with coriander leaves and serve immediately.

BLOW TORCHED SQUID
with Watercress Sauce

Being chefs, of course we love playing with blow torches. However if you don't have one you can cook the squid over a naked flame or on a barbecue – it needs an intensity of heat.

Depending on the time of year you can vary the watercress sauce, try using pears, apples or crab apples.

Serves 4

- 240g squid (60g each person), cut into long strips
- 6 tbsp rapeseed oil
- Half a garlic clove, puréed
- 2 cooked pears, puréed
- 100g watercress leaves
- 20g parsley, leaves only
- 100ml vegetable nage or good quality vegetable stock
- 2 tsp aioli (see glossary)

With a sharp knife, crisscross the squid on the inside membrane and slice into 3 cm long strips. Season with salt and pepper and place membrane side down on a surface that can take some heat, such as a baking tray.

Warm the rapeseed oil in a medium pan and sweat the garlic until soft but not brown, then add the watercress and parsley. When the leaves have wilted, remove from the heat and stir over iced water to chill rapidly.

When cold, place in a blender with the puréed pear, add nage or vegetable stock and liquidise at high speed to extract all the colour.

Season and strain through a fine sieve. Re-warm in a pan when needed, adding aioli to enrich the sauce.

Blow torch the squid until it curls and a blackened crisscross pattern has formed and serve with the sauce.

PAN-FRIED MACKEREL,
Fennel Purée & Rhubarb Chutney

Mackerel is a classic St. Ives fish. The sweet and sour aspects of rhubarb cut through the oiliness of mackerel really well here, as do the citrus notes of wood sorrel in the salad.

Serves 4

– 4 large mackerel, skin on and scaled
– 2 tbsp olive oil
– Salt & pepper

FENNEL PURÉE
– 1 bulb of fennel, finely sliced
– 2 tbsp butter
– 1 small shallot, finely sliced
– 50ml single cream
– Salt
– White pepper

SWEET & SOUR RHUBARB CHUTNEY
– 200g diced rhubarb
– 30g caster sugar
– 1 tsp white wine vinegar
– ½ tsp salt
– 25ml grenadine

SALAD
– 1 tbsp sumac
– 1 lemon
– 12 sprigs of wood sorrel
– 8 sprigs wild sorrel or spinach
  if not available
– 100g endive
– 2 tbsp extra virgin olive oil

First, make the rhubarb chutney. Bring the sugar, grenadine and white wine vinegar to the boil, add the rhubarb and cook for about 3 minutes - it still needs to have some firmness. Add salt to taste.

For the fennel purée, sweat the fennel in the butter with the shallots until very soft. Blitz till smooth and finish with the cream, salt and white pepper and set aside.

Place a large frying pan on a medium heat with the oil. Season the mackerel fillets. When the oil is hot, place the fillets skin side down, cook for 3 minutes then flip and cook for a further 1-2 minutes.

Get yourself a jar or cup, add the lemon juice, sumac and olive oil and give it a good mix before seasoning. Dress the salad.

Finally, place the mackerel fillets on top of the fennel purée, scatter over the salad leaves and serve with a spoonful of the rhubarb chutney.

COCONUT POACHED GURNARD

Gurnard can be a bit of a fiddly fish to work with, but it's very pretty, highly sustainable and they catch a lot of it in Cornwall. You could use red mullet if you can't get hold of gurnard.

Serves 4

- 4 gurnards, filleted
- 4 cans of coconut cream
- Juice of a lime
- 4 kaffir lime leaves
- 4 star anise
- 2 long peppers
- 2 tbsp fish sauce
- 2 tbsp palm sugar
- 1 tbsp grated ginger
- 2 red chillies, finely sliced
- 2 garlic cloves, smashed
- 2 lemon grass sticks, smashed

TO SERVE
- 250g of Jasmine rice
- 2 tsp ground long or black pepper
- 1 tsp black sesame seeds
- Mixed leaves served with Thai salad
  dressing (see glossary)
- Toasted coconut shavings
- Lime wedges

Combine all the poaching ingredients and bring to the boil. Strain into another pan, submerge the gurnard fillets in the poaching mix, cover and poach on a very low heat for 10 minutes until cooked.

Cover the jasmine rice with twice as much boiling water and rapidly boil for 10 minutes before straining. Grind the long (or black) pepper and the black sesame seeds in a pestle and mortar and stir through the cooked rice.

Serve with wedges of lime, Thai-dressed salad and toasted coconut shavings.

SCALLOPS
with Avocado Salsa & Dukkah Spice

Serves 4

– 12 large scallops, cleaned, roe removed (ask your fishmonger to do this)
– 12 scallops shells, cleaned and boiled for a few minutes
– 2 tomatoes
– 2 ripe avocados
– 1 red onion, very finely sliced
– 1 lemon
– A few sprigs of mint, finely chopped
– 2 tbsp extra virgin olive oil
– Salt and pepper
– Dukkah spice
  (see opposite)

Bring a small pan of water to a rolling boil. Cut the eye from the tomatoes and make a criss-cross incision on the opposite end of each. Drop the tomatoes into the boiling water for about 15-20 seconds or until the skin begins to peel back, then plunge into iced water. With a small knife, peel off the skins, cut them into quarters and remove the seeds. Cut the flesh into a small dice.

Peel the avocados, cut into small cubes and squeeze over the lemon juice to prevent from going brown.

Put the avocado and tomato into a bowl with the sliced red onion. Grate over the zest of the lemon, add the chopped mint, olive oil and season with salt and pepper. Season the scallops and sear in a frying pan until golden brown (about 2 minutes on each side).

Serve the cooked scallops in the shells with a generous spoonful of salsa and a sprinkling of the dukkah spice.

We use hand-dived scallops, which are much more ethical as they don't harm the sea floor.

DUKKAH SPICE

- 3 tbsp chopped hazelnuts
- 1 tbsp sesame seeds
- 2 tbsp coriander seeds
- 1 tbsp cumin seeds
- 1 tsp fennel seeds
- ½ tsp black peppercorns
- 1 tsp sea salt

Roast everything in a baking tray in a low oven (150°C) for about 25 minutes or until the spices and nuts are crisp and fragrant smelling, taking care not to let them burn. When cooled, grind in a pestle and mortar and store in an airtight jar.

CRISPY FRIED CUTTLEFISH
with Citrus White Miso

*We cook this with cuttlefish when it's
in season as it's local, plentiful and
the end result has a great texture,
but you can also use squid.*

Serves 4 as a starter

- 2 medium cuttlefish
  (each approx 150g cleaned weight)
- ½ cup cornflour
- ½ cup gram (chickpea) flour
- 1 tsp black spice mix (see glossary)
- Salt

- Citrus miso (see glossary)

Mix the flours together.

Heat a deep fat fryer or large saucepan filled with cooking oil until the temperature reaches 180–190°C.

Meanwhile, prepare the cuttlefish. Clean any gunk from inside the body, slit it up the side to unfold it, score the inside with a table knife, and cut into several triangle shaped pieces.

Dredge in the flour mix, dusting off any excess and fry till crispy and lightly golden brown, around 3-4 minutes. Carefully drain onto kitchen paper, season with salt and the black spice mix and toss together.

Serve with the citrus miso dipping sauce.

CORNISH SARDINES
with Red Onion, Rosemary & Lemon

*A really simple and
delicious dish, this
would also be fabulous
cooked on a barbecue.*

Serves 4

– 8 sardines
– 1 red onion, sliced
– 4 sprigs of rosemary
– 1 garlic clove, chopped
– 3 preserved lemons, thinly sliced
– 2 tbsp chopped parsley
– Juice of half a lemon
– 2 tbsp sherry vinegar
– 75ml olive oil
– Salt and pepper

Cornish new potatoes, to serve

Fill a pan with water, add a pinch of salt and the new potatoes. Bring to the boil and leave until tender, about 15 minutes from boiling point.

Meanwhile pour the olive oil into a large frying pan, big enough to fit 8 sardines. Put the pan on a medium to high heat so the sardines sizzle as they hit the pan. They should blister and turn brown.

Cook for about 3 minutes before flipping and adding the rosemary, garlic, red onions, sherry vinegar and preserved lemons. Cook for a further 2-3 minutes, without colouring too much.

When the sardines are just cooked, turn off the heat and add the lemon juice and parsley to finish.

Serve with new potatoes and the delicious pan juices.

THAI CRAB CAKES
with Sweet Chilli Sauce

An Asian twist on a crab cake, very fresh tasting and a world away from shop bought versions. This dish has been on our menu for nearly 10 years.

Serves 4-6 (makes 12 cakes)

- 500g white fish fillets, skinned and boned (cod or pollock work well)
- ½ onion, finely diced
- 2 cloves garlic, peeled and finely chopped
- 1 finger length red chilli, de-seeded, finely diced
- 1 tsp finely chopped lemongrass
- 1 kaffir lime leaf, finely chopped
- Sunflower oil
- 500g Maris Piper potatoes, peeled, boiled and mashed
- 250g picked white crab meat
- 250g brown crab meat
- 2 spring onions, finely sliced
- ½ bunch coriander, picked and roughly chopped
- 100g plain flour
- 3 eggs, beaten

CRUMB MIX
- 300g fresh white breadcrumbs
- 2 tbsp nigella seeds

- Sweet chilli sauce, to serve

Place the fish on a baking tray with a splash of oil, salt and pepper and roast in an oven at 200°C for about 20 minutes. Pour off any excess liquid from the tray then set aside to cool.

Sweat the onion, garlic, chilli, lemongrass and lime leaf in a little sunflower oil in a large pan, until soft and sweet but not coloured. Allow to cool.

In a large bowl, combine the onion mixture with the mashed potato. Flake in the white fish and add the brown and white crabmeat, coriander and spring onion. Season with salt to taste.

Refrigerate for at least an hour to give the mixture a chance to firm up. Meanwhile, mix together the ingredients for the crumb mix.

Next, divide the chilled mixture into 12 and shape into cakes weighing around 100g each.

Dip each cake in flour, beaten egg, then the crumb mix. Deep fry at 175°C until golden brown and crispy.

Serve with a salad dressed with Thai dressing and our sweet chilli sauce (see glossary).

We Float IV © Anthony Frost

CORNISH DASHI BROTH

Dashi is a Japanese stock base made from cured, smoked and dried bonito (a member of the tuna family) and dried konbu seaweed. These two ingredients are then rehydrated and simmered in water, which produces a base stock for most Japanese broths, including miso soup.

Our kitchen is proud to have created its own Cornish version, using mackerel, which is similar to bonito, and dulse, a purplish seaweed which grows on nearby rocks. We semi-cure and smoke the mackerel and then dehydrate it along with the dulse.

Serves 4

DASHI BASE
- 50g dried mackerel (or bonito) flakes
- 25g dried dulse (or konbu) seaweed
- 2.5 litres of water

TO SERVE
- 12 mussels, de-bearded and washed
- 4 scallops
- 8 surf clams
- 1 washed head of pak choi
- 100g rice noodles
- 1 chilli, de-seeded and finely sliced
- 2 tsp grated ginger

Bring all the dashi base ingredients slowly to the boil and then simmer until the flakes fall from the top to the bottom of the pan. Set aside to settle and then strain.

Add the ingredients of your choice to form a soup (the list opposite is just a suggestion). Place your chosen ingredients in the dashi broth and simmer for 3 minutes.

Season with a touch of soy sauce and serve in deep bowls with a soup spoon and chop sticks.

SWEET & SOUR MUSSELS

This is our Asian interpretation of Moules Marinière. We use mussels from Fowey, which are balanced nicely with aromatic spices and chilli, tamarind and coconut.

If you don't have the time to make the chilli and tamarind jam, you can cheat using a combination of tamarind pulp and sweet chilli sauce.

Serves 4

– 1kg cleaned, closed mussels
– 2 tbsp tamarind jam (see glossary)
– 150ml coconut milk
– 100ml chicken stock
– 1 lemon grass stalk, halved lengthways
– 2 lime leaves
– 3 leaves of bok choi

TO SERVE
– Handful coriander leaves
– Toasted coconut shavings
– 1 lime

Place 2 tbsp of tamarind jam in a pre-heated wok with the chicken stock, lime leaves and lemon grass and bring to the boil.

Add the mussels. When they're nearly all opened, throw in the bok choi and continue to cook until all of the mussels have fully opened.

Discard any unopened mussels, scatter over the coriander leaves and coconut shavings and serve with wedges of lime.

White balsamic, homemade tartare sauce and rosemary and garlic infused chips all lift this dish above your average takeaway.

FISH & CHIPS,
Aussie Style

Serves 4

- 4 x 200g haddock fillets, pinboned
- 500g Maris Piper potatoes
- 1 litre sunflower oil
- 2 sprigs of rosemary
- 1 bulb of garlic
- Sea salt

BATTER
- 200g self raising flour
- 50g cornflour
- 300ml good lager
  (Skinners Cornish is our favourite)
- ½ tsp baking powder
- A pinch of sea salt

TO SERVE
- 1 lemon, cut into wedges
- White balsamic vinegar
- Tartare sauce (see glossary)

First peel your potatoes and cut them into chips about 1cm thick. Blanch them in a deep pan of boiling salted water for 3 minutes, then carefully drain, making sure they don't fall apart. Lay on a tray, sprinkle with salt and place in the fridge to cool.

Heat the sunflower oil in your fryer or a safe pan to 175°C. Preheat the oven to 100°C.

Meanwhile make your tartare sauce by combining all the ingredients in a bowl. Keep in the fridge until you need it.

Whisk all the batter ingredients together in a bowl.

Fry the chips in batches with the garlic and rosemary. Do not overcrowd the fryer and fry until they are all beautifully golden brown, this should take 3-4 minutes. Drain on kitchen paper and salt generously before putting in the oven to keep warm.

Pat the fish dry with kitchen paper. Dip one fillet into the batter before carefully lowering into the oil, working away from you so you don't splash yourself. Repeat with the next fillet and fry for 4 minutes until golden and crisp. Drain on kitchen paper and place in the oven with the chips while you fry the next 2 fillets.

Serve your fish and chips with a wedge of lemon, white balsamic vinegar, salt and a bowl of tartare sauce.

CRAB RISOTTO

Rather than stirring the crab meat through the risotto, here it sits underneath it so you get a nice contrast in textures. Make sure you bring the crab mixture up to room temperature before serving.

Serves 4

CRAB MIXTURE
- 100g picked white crab meat
- ¼ bunch finely chopped chives
- 3 sprigs dill, chopped
- 3 sprigs tarragon, chopped
- Juice of 1 lemon
- Extra virgin olive oil

- 350ml light chicken stock (you may not need all of this)
- 4 tbsp mild olive oil
- ¼ onion, peeled and finely diced
- ½ stick celery, trimmed and finely diced
- ¼ bulb fennel, trimmed and finely diced
- 125g risotto rice, preferably canaroli
- 25ml dry vermouth
- 20g freshly grated parmesan
- 30g diced butter
- A splash of limoncello
- Handful of basil leaves
- Salt and pepper

Pick through the crabmeat to make sure it's free from any shell. Place in a bowl and add the chives, dill and tarragon. Season to taste with salt, pepper, lemon juice and extra virgin olive oil. Put to one side.

Bring the chicken stock to a light simmer in a saucepan.

Heat the olive oil in a large, heavy-based pan over a medium heat and add the onion, celery and fennel. Stir regularly with a wooden spoon, cooking until slightly softened without colouring. When there is no more steam being given off by the vegetables, add the rice and toss everything around.

Add the vermouth and allow it to bubble away. When it has almost completely evaporated, pour on enough hot chicken stock so that the rice is completely submerged. Turn down the heat and allow the stock to cook, stirring constantly. Once this stock has been completely absorbed, remove the pan from the heat.

Taste a grain of rice – it should be slightly al dente but not chalky – if it is too raw, add a little more stock and heat whilst stirring until al dente.

Remove the risotto from the pan and finish by stirring in the parmesan, butter, limoncello and torn basil leaves. Taste and season with salt and pepper.

Distribute the dressed crab evenly between 4 plates, creating a circular mound in the centre of each. Spoon the risotto over the top so each mound of crab is completely covered. Serve immediately.

CORNISH CRAB & MUSSEL LINGUINE

Serves 4

- 120g picked white crabmeat
- 350g dried linguine
- 100ml mild olive oil
- 40 mussels
- 2 red chillies, deseeded and finely diced
- 4 cloves of garlic, peeled and finely chopped
- 300ml light chicken stock
- Juice of 2 lemons
- ½ a bunch of flat leaf parsley, roughly chopped
- Salt and pepper

First pick through the crabmeat to make sure it's free from any bits of shell. Scrub the mussels under running water, remove any grit and pull off the little 'beards'.

Bring a large pan of salted water to the boil, add the linguine and cook as per instructions until al dente.

Meanwhile, in a pan large enough to take all the mussels comfortably, heat the olive oil, add the mussels and stir until they begin to open.

Next, add the chilli and garlic and cook till softened without browning, stirring regularly. Add the chicken stock and lemon juice to the pan and bring to the boil.

Drain the pasta, reserving a little of the cooking water. Add the drained pasta to the mussels with the parsley and crabmeat and toss together until everything is evenly mixed. Taste and season. Loosen with a little of the cooking water if the pasta looks too dry.

This classic combination of simple ingredients works so well with the crab and mussels here.

Using fish stock can be a bit strong and make the crab overpowering so we opt for chicken stock, which gives a more rounded flavour.

*Lobster is best when
served simply, like this.*

CORNISH LOBSTER
*with Vanilla Mayonnaise
& Citrus Salad*

Serves 4

- 2 live lobsters, 700-800g
- 125ml mayonnaise (see glossary)
- Juice of 1 lime
- ½ vanilla pod

SALAD
- 1 cucumber
- 1 bulb fennel
- 1 grapefruit, segmented
- 200g mixed baby leaves
- Foraged herbs (or if unavailable, a mix of chives - ¼ bunch, tarragon - 4 sprigs and dill - 4 sprigs)
- Sea salt
- Juice of ½ a lemon
- 4 tbsp good olive oil

TO SERVE
- 2 lemons, cut in half

Chill your lobsters in the freezer to de-sensitize them for at least half an hour. Preheat your oven to 250°C.

Scrape the seeds from the vanilla pod and mix with the mayonnaise and lime juice. Divide between four small ramekins.

Cut the cucumber in half lengthways and remove the seeds with a spoon. Slice at an angle into slithers, approximately 3mm thick.

Trim the stalk off the fennel and slice very thinly through the circumference with a knife or mandolin. Mix the fennel slices, cucumber, grapefruit segments, herbs and baby leaves in a bowl. Remove the lobsters from the freezer and with a large, sharp

knife, split them lengthways, making sure a clean blow goes through the head first. Remove the coral (greeny pulp from the head area).

Place the lobsters on a baking tray and pour over a little olive oil, salt and pepper. Cook for 10–12 minutes in the oven, until the flesh has lost its opacity.

Season the salad, toss with lemon juice and olive oil and divide equally between 4 plates. Place a ramekin of vanilla mayonnaise, half a lemon and some salad beside each half of lobster.

MONKFISH CURRY

Our interpretation of Indonesian and Thai flavours, this monkfish curry has become one of the Café's signature dishes.

Serves 4

- 2 sweet potatoes (roughly 200g each),
  peeled and cut into thick (3cm) slices
- 1 tbsp sesame oil
- 1 tbsp sunflower oil
- 600g cleaned monkfish tails, cut into
  chunks (4cm x 4cm cubes)
- 8 raw shelled prawns
- 12-16 mussels (depending on size)
- 4 tbsp curry paste
  (see recipe below)
- 200ml chicken stock
- 4 kaffir lime leaves, fresh or dried
- 4 star anise
- 800ml coconut milk
- 2 tbsp tamarind jam
  (see glossary)
- 12 cherry tomatoes
- 12 bok choi leaves, sliced into 3cm strips
- Fish sauce, to taste

CURRY PASTE
- 4 garlic cloves, roughly chopped
- ¼ tbsp shrimp paste
- 2 long red chillies, roughly chopped
- 60g fresh turmeric or 3 tsp dried
- ½ tbsp chopped ginger
- 1 lemon grass stem, bashed and roughly
  chopped
- 2 spring onions, roughly chopped
- 1 plum tomato, roughly chopped
- 2 bird's eye chillies
- 4g fresh galangal (or ginger), tough
  outer skin removed and roughly
  chopped
- 1 tsp coriander seeds
- 3 tsp palm sugar
- ¼ tsp nutmeg
- ¼ bunch coriander stems, roughly
  chopped

Blitz all the ingredients for the curry paste with a stick blender.

Place the sweet potatoes on a baking tray, toss with a little oil, salt and pepper and cook at 180°C for about 30 minutes, or until just soft to the touch.

In a wok or large saucepan (25cm in diameter) heat the sunflower oil and sesame oil. Add the monkfish cubes to the hot pan and cook on a high heat until light golden brown.

Add the curry paste to the pan, lower the heat slightly and cook for about 3 minutes. Throw in the prawns and mussels, add the chicken stock and simmer until it has reduced by half.

Add the coconut milk, lime leaves, star anise and tamarind jam, turn down the heat and simmer for a further 3–4 mins.

Add the cherry tomatoes, bok choi and sweet potato and cook until tender (around another 3–4 mins). Finish with fish sauce to taste and serve with jasmine rice.

PAN ROASTED HAKE
with Razor Clams, Almond Paste, Celeriac & Bacon

*Hake is the fish of St.Ives
- local people are even
known as hakes! A very
underrated fish, we always
try to put it on the menu
when it's in season.*

Serves 4

– 4 x 175g hake fillets
– 12 fresh razor clams, washed under
  cold water
– 200g thick bacon, cut into cubes
– 1 handful of hairy bittercress
  or rocket
– 250g spinach
– 2 tbsp rapeseed oil
– 1 small glass of white wine

ALMOND PASTE
– 100g blanched whole toasted almonds
– 250ml semi-skimmed milk
– ½ tsp sugar
– 1 bay leaf
– Large pinch of salt

CELERIAC PURÉE
– 1 celeriac - grated
– Milk to cover
– 2 tbsp of cream
– Knob of butter

For the almond paste, combine the milk, bay leaf, salt and sugar and bring to the boil. Boil for about 3 minutes and then blitz in a liquidiser until smooth. Pass through a sieve and place in the fridge to set.

Meanwhile, make the celeriac purée. Cover the celeriac with milk in a pan and add 1 tsp of salt. Boil until very soft, then strain through a fine sieve. Press with the back of a spoon to extract as much liquid as possible. Heat the cream and melt the butter. This bit is best done whilst the celeriac is still warm.

Put the cream, butter and celeriac in a blender and purée until completely smooth. Season to taste, set aside and cover with foil.

Heat the oil in a heavy-based frying pan and cook the hake skin side down for around 2-3 minutes each side, or until cooked through. Remove, add the bacon cubes and crisp up until golden brown.

Add the white wine and the razor clams to the pan and cover. Cook until they open, about 2 minutes. Remove from their shells, roughly chop the clams and add back to the pan with spinach and hake. Leave for 30 seconds to warm through and let the spinach wilt.

Slice the almond paste, smear the purée and place on a plate along with the ingredients from the clam pan. Garnish with the hairy bittercress or rocket.

WHOLE BAKED SEA BASS
with Salt Crust

This is a great way of cooking whole fish or even whole birds like chicken, as the salt pastry crust keeps in all the moisture and flavour. There's also a real wow factor in presenting and opening this at the table - perfect sharing food for a celebration.

Serves 4

– One large wild sea bass or 4 smaller
  x 300g bass, gutted, scaled, fins and
  gills removed
– 330g rock salt
– 330g fine sea salt
– 5 cups (800g) plain flour
– 350ml water
– ½ bulb fennel, trimmed and thinly
  sliced
– 1 lemon, thinly sliced
– 4 sprigs parsley
– 2 egg yolks, beaten

Mix the salts and flour together in a large bowl. Add the water gradually, mixing with your hands until it comes together to form a dough – you may need to add a little more water if the mixture is too dry. Wrap the dough in cling film and refrigerate for at least an hour.

Pat the fish dry and stuff them with the parsley, fennel and lemon. Keep in the fridge until you are ready.

Preheat the oven to 180°C. On a floured surface, roll out the dough to a thickness of a pound coin and cut out 2 fish-shaped sheets (or 8 if using individual fish) 1-2 cm wider then the fish, but a little shorter as you want to leave the head and tail poking out.

Place the fish on one of the pastry sheets and cover with the second one. Squeeze the edges of the pastry together where they join to seal. Leave the head and tail poking out. Place on a baking tray and brush the pastry with the beaten egg yolks.

Bake for 20 minutes then remove from the oven and rest for 5 minutes, before cutting open the pastry at the table.

Serve with Cornish new potatoes, a green salad and some salsa verde (see glossary).

FISH
Glossary

Brill

Cod

Seabass

Gurnard

Hake

Plaice

John Dory

Halibut

Haddock

Lemon sole

Mackerel

Turbot

Brill

Similar in flavour to turbot but earthier and less sweet, brill is a good and cheaper alternative.
Works with: **mushrooms, red wine, Jerusalem artichokes, tarragon, rosemary, thyme and braised beef.**

Gurnard

A memorable fish to look at, gurnard is often overlooked as it can be quite fiddly to prepare, but it has a lovely rich meaty flesh.
Works with: **bouillabaisse, orange, fennel, star anise, waxy potatoes, chilli and ginger.**

John Dory

Also known as St Peter's fish, John Dory is defined by its 'evil eye', the unique dark spot on its body. Firm and meaty yet delicate enough to work well with a wide range of flavours.
Works with: **anything from strong Asian dishes, to lighter flavours such as white crab and dill.**

Lemon Sole

Light, soft and delicate, we often serve lemon sole whole or in fillets with just a little brown lemon butter and fresh herbs.
Works with: **saffron, white crab, dill and parsley. Avoid strong flavours.**

Cod

The most well known fish in the ocean, cod has suffered from severe overfishing and stocks now needs to be managed very carefully, especially in the North Sea.
Works with: **citrus, red spices, creamy sauces, fresh green vegetables, olive oil, garlic, soft green herbs.**

Hake

The fish of St.Ives, hake is prolific in the local waters. An underrated fish, it has a soft white flesh with a light flake and a little sweetness. Hake is a great replacement for cod and also works well in batter.
Works with: **similar flavours to cod and haddock.**

Halibut

One of the bottom dwelling giants which are caught in the depths of the Celtic and North Sea, halibut can grow up to 2 metres in length. Its flesh is firm and light yet meaty, pairing very well with stong flavours.
Works with: **chanterelles, foie gras, truffles, rosemary, braised red onions, red wine, thyme and sage.**

Mackerel

A most adaptable fish. We use it for pâtés, smoked, grilled, pan fried and Japanese style, served raw. One rule you must remember: only ever eat mackerel on the day it is caught!
Works with: **sharper flavours like rhubarb, pomegranate and sumac.**

Sea Bass

Another of our favourite local fish to cook and eat, we get the best line-caught sea bass delivered to our doorstep just a few hours after being caught. Can be grilled, poached, steamed and pan-fried, all producing great results.
Works with: **soy and citrus; unusual flavours such as vanilla and saffron.**

Plaice

Can be used like lemon sole, but has a slightly meatier texture. Should be avoided when spawning in winter as the roe can quadruple in size and the flesh goes mushy.
Works with: **Asian flavours; also good crispy fried.**

Haddock

Our favourite for fish and chips (particularly the smaller fish), haddock is also great when smoked.
Works with: **cream, leek, garlic, parsley and dill.**

Turbot

Along with Dover sole, turbot is often deemed to be the prize or trophy fish. It has a firm but beautifully flavoured flesh that can truly melt in the mouth if cooked correctly. We prefer to serve turbot on the bone, which helps to retain its juices.
Works with: **the same flavours as brill.**

SCALLOPS
with Bacon, Cauliflower Purée & Salted Grapes

Scallops are great to work with because their rich creamy texture can marry a lot of different flavours together, as they do to great effect in this dish.

Serves 4

- 12 fresh scallops
- 250g bacon or pancetta
- Knob of butter
- 1 tbsp olive oil

CAULIFLOWER PURÉE
- 1 shallot
- ½ a clove of garlic
- 1 small cauliflower (only use tender florets)
- Pinch of fresh grated nutmeg
- Full cream milk to cover, about 250ml
- Knob of butter

SALTED GRAPES
- 24 seedless red or green grapes, peeled
- 1 tsp caster sugar
- Olive oil
- 1 tsp salt

Preheat oven to 120°C.

Combine the grapes, sugar, 20ml olive oil and sea salt in a bowl and stir to coat. Place on a lightly oiled wire rack and cook until semi-dried (40-45 minutes), set aside to cool.

For the cauliflower purée, sweat the shallots and garlic until soft and tender, add the cauliflower, cover with milk and poach until tender. Strain off the milk, blitz the cauliflower and slowly add some milk back until you have a purée consistency. Add the grated nutmeg and finish with a touch of butter to make it silky.

Fry the bacon or pancetta in a large non-stick frying pan over a medium-high heat for 4-6 minutes until the fat crisps, turning once.

Remove the bacon, pat dry with kitchen paper, place on a baking tray and keep warm in the oven. Add a knob of butter, cook the scallops for 1-2 minutes on each side depending on their size, until golden-brown on the outside but tender within. Season.

Place the scallops on the cauliflower purée, scatter over the bacon and the salted grapes.

SEA BASS
with Crab Fritters
& Chilli Ponzu

Another favourite on the menu, this uses the same mixture as the Thai crab cakes, but rather than being crumbed, it's battered in a light tempura.

Serves 4

– 2 x 500g sea bass filleted – 4 fillets
– Crab cake mix - see Thai crab cakes
  and halve the quantities

TEMPURA BATTER
– 100g plain flour
– 100ml sparkling water
– 1 tbsp cornflour
– Sea salt

TO SERVE
– 100ml ponzu (see glossary)
– 1 red chilli, finely sliced

Make up the Thai crab cake mixture, using half the quantities of the recipe on page 38.

Refrigerate the mixture for at least an hour so it firms up. It can then be divided into 20 little balls.

Make your tempura batter by whisking the sparkling water into the flour, salt and cornflour. Dip each ball into the batter and deep fry at 180°C for 3 minutes or so until golden brown. Keep warm in a low oven.

Sear the bass fillets in a large frying pan for around 3 minutes each side, skin side down first. Whilst it's cooking, add the finely sliced chilli to the ponzu, keeping the seeds if you prefer some heat.

Serve the sea bass with the fritters, salad dressed with Thai salad dressing (see glossary) and the chilli ponzu.

**GRILL COPY2
TICKET : 36
TABLE 8/ 2 CL
CLERK 10 GEORGIE
1 JOHN DORY
1 JOHN DORY
one
less chilli
in salad
27-06-2011 8:11:56 TABLE 8
HANDY : 1

WHOLE LEMON SOLE
with Samphire, Crab & Verbena

Serves 4

- 4 whole lemon soles, with the fins and roe removed
- ½ cup of samphire
- 1 cup picked white crabmeat
- 1 tbsp fresh lemon verbena, torn
- 1 tomato, de-seeded and diced
- 1 litre of fish stock (see glossary)
- 6-8 new potatoes (depending on size), cooked and skinned
- 2 tbsp butter
- Salt and pepper
- 1 cup (250ml) of white wine

De-scale the fish, or ask your fishmonger to help you with this.

Heat a splash of rapeseed or olive oil in a large frying pan, place the fish presentation side down and cook for a few minutes. Turn the fish over and repeat the process until the fish is golden on both sides. Remove the fish and place on a baking tray for later.

De-glaze the frying pan with the white wine and add the fish stock. Reduce the liquid by two thirds, then add the cooked potatoes, diced tomato and samphire. Let the mixture simmer for a few minutes, stirring occasionally, then slowly add the butter to emulsify the sauce.

Place the fish back in a hot oven for a couple of minutes. While the fish is re-heating, stir the crab and verbena into the sauce at the last minute. Place the sole on a plate, cover with the sauce and serve immediately.

Samphire grows on the rocks nearby so in spring and summer we try to use it as much as we can. Lemon verbena has a wonderfully pungent citrus smell that goes so well with the lemon sole and crab.

The Porthminster garden sits on the hillside opposite the Café. What started as a small herb garden - no more than 2 by 2 metres - has grown every year to become an invaluable source of produce for the Café.

We grow up to 50 different types of fruit, vegetables and herbs at any one time. From rhubarb in early spring to courgette flowers during the summer, produce from the garden is used in our dishes every day.

We owe a huge thanks to Jim and Julie Horn for their brilliance in initially transforming the space, and to Davey Walker, who has cultivated the garden into its current abundant state.

Two fantastic ingredients – the finest white anchovies from Spain and sage, which grows relentlessly in our garden.

SAGE & ANCHOVY FRITTERS

Serves 4

– 12 cleaned white anchovies
 (boquerones)
– 24 fresh sage leaves
– 12 wooden or bamboo skewers
– 1 litre of vegetable oil

FOR THE BEER BATTER
– 250g self-raising flour, plus extra
 for dusting
– 80g cornflour
– 300ml cold lager
– ½ tsp baking powder
– Pinch of salt

TO SERVE
– Lemon mayonnaise (see glossary)
– Lemon wedges

For the beer batter, sieve all the dry ingredients into a large bowl and mix well. Make a well in the centre and pour in the cold beer. Whisk lightly, making sure there are no lumps and set aside in the fridge until ready.

Turn the deep fat fryer on to 190°C, or if you don't have one place the oil into a large heavy-bottomed pan and set over a medium heat. Drop in a sage leaf to test the heat - if it bubbles a lot and turns golden it's ready to use.

Skewer each of your sticks with a sage leaf, followed by an anchovy and then another sage leaf. Repeat this using all skewers. Roll the anchovies in the extra flour until well covered, this will help the batter to stick.

Dip each skewer into the beer batter and fry until golden, about 2-3 minutes. You may need to do this in 2 batches. Move the anchovies around every minute or so to ensure they are evenly cooked.

Drain onto kitchen paper and serve with lemon mayonnaise and a few wedges of lemon.

PARMESAN CRÈME BRÛLÉE
with Asparagus Soldiers

Serves 4

– 1 cup (250ml) double cream
– 160g freshly grated Parmesan
  cheese
– 3 large egg yolks
– Pinch salt
– 12 asparagus spears

Preheat the oven to 180°C. Boil a kettle of water. Place 4 x 6-ounce ramekins in a roasting pan with sides at least 2 inches high.

Heat the double cream in a saucepan over a medium heat. Just as it starts to bubble at the edges, stir in half of the cheese, keeping half back for the topping. Cook for 2-4 minutes, stirring constantly, until the cheese has melted and the mixture is smooth. Reduce the heat so the mixture does not come to a boil.

If you'd like to produce ultra-smooth brûlées, push the mixture through a fine mesh sieve at this point into a large measuring jug.

Whisk the egg yolks and salt in a small jug or bowl. Mix in a small amount of the hot cream mixture to temper the egg yolks, then pour all of the mixture into the large measuring jug, stirring to combine.

Divide the mixture between the ramekins. Pour enough of the just boiled water into the roasting pan so that the water is three-quarters of the way up the sides of the ramekins (forming a bain-marie, or water bath). Cover the pan tightly with plastic wrap and bake for about 35 minutes or until the custards are just set, with a slight jiggle at the centre. The internal temperature of the custards should register 171°C on an instant-read thermometer.

Discard the plastic wrap. Use tongs or a wide spatula to transfer the ramekins to a heatproof surface to cool.

Place the remaining parmesan cheese in 4 small circles (the same size as the top of the ramekins) on a baking tray lined with greaseproof paper. You can use a pastry cutter to get the right size and shape. Place under a pre-heated grill and cook until golden brown. Leave to cool then remove with a spatula and place on top of the brûlées.

Serve with steamed or grilled asparagus spears for dipping. You could also try wrapping the asparagus in parma ham or pancetta.

This savoury crème brûlée is a fun and different way of serving asparagus. The brûlées taste best on the same day they are made, but they can also be baked a day in advance and refrigerated. Bring to room temperature, then finish with the topping just before they are served.

Courgette flowers grow from mid-June until August. They're exceptionally easy to grow – some mornings we'll pick 30 and there'll be another 30 back by the afternoon.

You can stuff courgette flowers with whatever you fancy. A few Porthminster favourites are goat's cheese and pickled walnuts, and Cornish ricotta with semi-dried tomatoes.

TEMPURA COURGETTE FLOWERS

Serves 4

– 12 courgette flowers, washed to remove
  any dirt or bugs
– 2 litres sunflower oil

FILLING
– 1 tbsp basil, finely chopped
– 1 tbsp chives, finely snipped
– 1 tbsp parsley, finely chopped
– 200g ricotta
– 200g pecorino
– 6 semi-dried tomatoes
– Salt and pepper

TEMPURA BATTER
– 85g plain flour
– 1 heaped tbsp cornflour
– ½ tsp fine sea salt
– 200ml ice-cold soda water
– A few ice cubes

Heat the oil to about 190°C or until a cube of bread turns brown in 45-60 seconds.

Add the herbs to the ricotta and stir in the pecorino, season with pepper and taste before adding salt.

Fill each of the flowers with about 3 teaspoons of the ricotta mixture and twist the tips of the petals to secure the filling.

Make the batter by putting the flour, cornflour, and salt in a large bowl. Give it a whisk to remove any lumps. Slowly add the soda water and then the ice cubes, whisking as you pour, to achieve a batter with the consistency of single cream.

Dip the flowers in the batter just before using, shake off any excess then slowly lower into the hot oil. Don't overcrowd the pan, 3-4 at a time is usually enough. Fry for about 2-3 minutes or until golden and crisp and then drain on kitchen paper. Repeat with the remaining flowers and serve immediately.

LEEK & POTATO SOUP
with Black Spice

This recipe came about completely by accident, when the black spice mixture for the crispy cuttlefish fell into a pan of leek and potato soup. It works surprisingly well - the warm spices provide a lovely contrast to the mild and soothing soup.

Serves 4

- Olive oil
- A knob of butter
- 1 large onion, peeled and finely chopped
- 2 leeks, washed, trimmed and finely sliced
- 2 cloves of garlic, peeled and chopped
- 800g Maris Piper potatoes, peeled and chopped into small chunks
- 1 litre of good hot vegetable stock
- 300ml double cream or crème fraîche
- A small bunch of chives, finely chopped
- Black spice (see glossary)

Heat a large pan and add the olive oil and the butter. Add the onions, leeks and garlic and cook on a low heat for 20 minutes, until they are soft and sweet but not coloured.

Once the leeks are ready, add the cubed potatoes and cover in the hot stock, season with salt and pepper and bring to the boil. Turn the heat down and simmer for 30 minutes until the potatoes are soft and break easily. Add a little more hot stock if the soup looks too thick.

Once the potatoes are soft, blitz the soup until smooth. Stir in the cream and the chopped chives and top with a sprinkling of black spice.

HALLOUMI AND BEETROOT SALAD
with Wild Sorrel, Sumac & Orange

Serves 4 as a starter,
or 2 for lunch

- 4 small beetroots
- 4 sprigs of thyme
- 400g halloumi cheese
- 2 tbsp rapeseed oil
- 1 tsp sumac
- 1 cup sorrel, preferably wild
- 1 orange
- 200g mixed salad leaves
- ½ red onion, finely sliced
- ½ bulb of fennel, finely sliced
- Balsamic vinegar
- Extra virgin olive oil
- Salt and pepper

Preheat the oven to 200°C.

Clean the beetroots under cold water, taking care not to pierce the skin. Wrap them in foil with the thyme, a splash of the rapeseed oil, salt and pepper and cook them in the oven until they are soft, approximately 45 minutes.

When they have cooled a little, peel the beetroots and set to one side. While they are cooling, peel the orange, segment half of it and reserve these segments to add to the salad. Place the remaining segments in a blender, along with 2 beetroots and 1 tbsp of rapeseed oil. Blend until smooth and then season with salt and pepper.

Cut the other 2 beetroots into the desired shapes for the salad. Wash the sorrel and mixed salad leaves and put them in a bowl with the beetroot, fennel, red onion and orange. Dress the salad with balsamic vinegar, olive oil and sumac.

Cut the halloumi into 1cm squares, add a splash of rapeseed oil to a hot frying pan and when it begins to smoke, add the halloumi and fry until golden, turning occasionally.

Finally smear the beetroot purée onto the plates, arrange the salad in the middle and serve with the halloumi on top.

The beetroot and citrus in this salad balance really nicely with the salty and rich halloumi cheese.

GOAT'S CHEESE TARTS
with Rocket Pesto

*An impressive but simple
vegetarian main course.*

Serves 4

- 400g matured goat's cheese (4 x 100g individual rounds or cut from a log)
- 2 small sweet potatoes (about 400g total)
- 4 fresh filo pastry sheets
- 100g unsalted butter, melted
- 2 leeks (white and pale green part only), thinly sliced
- 100g roasted red pepper, cut into strips (jarred is fine)
- 12 semi-dried tomatoes
- Rocket pesto (see glossary)
- Rocket and balsamic vinegar, to serve

Preheat oven to 180°C. Place the sweet potato in a roasting pan. Bake for 30 minutes or until tender. When cool enough to handle, halve lengthways, scoop out the flesh and set aside.

Lay 1 filo sheet on a work surface and brush well with melted butter. Top with another sheet of filo, then more butter until all the pastry is used. Cut the pastry into 4 x 15cm squares, then use to line 4 x 1-cup muffin holes. Bake for 5 minutes or until golden.

Meanwhile, place the remaining butter and leeks in a large pan over medium heat and cook, stirring, for 10 minutes or until soft but not brown. Divide the leeks, sweet potato, red pepper strips and semi-dried tomatoes among the tart shells. Top with the cheese rounds. Place back in the oven for 8 minutes, until the tarts are heated through and the cheese is golden brown on top.

Serve each tart with 1 tbsp of rocket pesto on top and some rocket, drizzled with balsamic.

Before every service at the Café, we usually have what's called the 'forage run', where one of the chefs runs up around the coastal path to gather lots of wild herbs. There's such a huge variety of wild produce in this part of Cornwall. We're incredibly lucky to have it so close to hand.

Have a bit of a closer look next time you're near a hedgerow or cliff path, you might be surprised at what you find. The beauty of foraging is that what's on offer is constantly changing with the seasons – and it's free!

WILD HERB
Glossary

Wild sorrel

Mustard cress

Wood sorrel

Rock samphire

wild spearmint

Pennywort

wild garlic

Rosehips

Sloes

Wild sorrel

This is the wild herb we most commonly use in the kitchen, especially in salads. Similar to wood sorrel but with a stronger flavour. Good with fish and salty cheese. There are lots of things which look similar - it's the long red stem you're looking for.

Wood sorrel

Looks a bit like clover, with an intense, citrussy flavour that goes very well with fish. This is probably our favourite of the two types of wild sorrel, but it does like to hide.

Wild spearmint

Has an absolutely incredible fresh smell, perfect for a soothing tea or summer ice cream. We find this amongst lots of nettles – part of the hazards of foraging!

Wild garlic

These little white bulbs become rampant in early spring and perfume the coast path. Wild garlic is really useful as you can use the flower, the stem and the bulb. Has flavours of both onion and garlic, and also chestnut. Delicious served with beef or salmon, they're also good pickled.

Mustard cress

These pretty yellow flowers dot the landscape everywhere here in spring. They have a really nice mild mustard flavour, with a hint of horseradish. Unsurprisingly they go very well with beef – great on an open steak sandwich.

Rock samphire

There are two types of samphire, marsh samphire and rock samphire. Rock samphire has a stronger, more aromatic flavour. Great with seafood, but try it with lamb as well.

Pennywort

Pennywort has three seasons, winter, spring and autumn. It looks a bit like a green chanterelle mushroom and has a nice, slightly bitter flavour to liven up salads.

Rosehips

We use these in desserts sometimes, but you have to take the skins off and cook them well with quite a lot of sugar. Rosehips are very high in vitamin C - rosehip preserve used to be given to convicts being taken to Australia to keep scurvy levels down.

Sloes

There's a sloe tree right next to the café. Around late September/ early October they'll start to ripen. We make sloe gin with them, which we sell at Christmas time.

Serves 6

- ½ small onion, finely diced
- ½ stalk celery, finely diced
- ½ bulb fennel, finely diced
- 50ml Noilly Prat or other dry vermouth
- 1 litre of simmering vegetable stock
- 500g canaroli or arborio rice
- 2 tbsp olive oil
- 1 courgette, diced
- 1 cup broad beans
- 1 cup fresh oregano, basil and mint, chopped
- 1 tsp chives
- 1 small lemon, juiced
- 10 tbsp parmesan cheese
- 5 tbsp mascarpone cheese
- A small handful of basil leaves, torn

We created this risotto to embrace the variety of vegetables we grow in the spring and summer months in the garden. You can vary the green vegetables depending on the time of year: chard, watercress and broad beans are good in spring, then courgettes and peas later on in summer.

Add the oil to a saucepan and sweat the onion, celery and fennel until soft. Add the rice and toss until the rice is coated and hot to touch. Do not stir the mixture and make sure the rice doesn't colour.

Add the Noilly Prat and let it evaporate, then cover the rice with 500ml of the stock. Heat slowly, stirring to encourage the starch to come out of the rice.

Keep adding hot stock and stirring for another 10-12 minutes. Squeeze the rice between your fingers: in the centre there should be 2 small white starchy dots. If this is correct your rice is nearly finished, if not add a little more stock and keep stirring until 2 dots are achieved.

Add the courgette, beans, chopped herbs and lemon juice. Cook for a further 3 minutes, stirring and adding any remaining stock if necessary.

Remove from the heat, leave for 2 minutes then return to the heat, stirring rapidly for a couple of minutes. Take off the heat, add the mascarpone and the basil, then stir in the parmesan. The rice should be al dente in texture. Serve immediately.

SUMMER VEGETABLE RISOTTO

TOMATO & AUBERGINE PASTA

Serves 4

– 400g linguine
– Parmesan cheese, to serve

NAPOLI SAUCE
– 1 large onion, finely chopped
– 4 cloves of garlic, finely chopped
– 3 tbsp tomato purée
– 1 cup olive oil
– 1 cup chopped basil and oregano
– 12 ripe tomatoes
– A pinch of salt
– A pinch of sugar
– A splash of red wine vinegar

RELISH OF SPICY AUBERGINE
– 2 large aubergines
– 1 tomato, chopped
– 1 onion, finely chopped
– 5g butter
– 5g fresh red chilli, finely sliced
– 5g garlic, finely sliced
– 5g ginger
– Zest of 1 lemon
– Juice of ½ a lemon
– 10ml balsamic vinegar
– 2 tbsp olive oil
– A small handful of coriander, chopped

Sweat the onions gently in the olive oil in a saucepan until see through, then add the garlic and cook for a further 5 minutes. Add the tomato purée and cook for another 5 minutes until the tomato paste is cooked out.

Add the tomatoes, cover the saucepan and simmer very gently for 1 - 1 ½ hours. When the tomatoes have softened, stir the sauce occasionally. When the sauce has thickened, blitz and pass the sauce through a sieve to remove the seeds.

Add the chopped herbs and the salt, sugar and vinegar to balance the flavour.

Cut the aubergine into 2cm squares, salt, then leave for 10 minutes. Rinse the aubergines in cold water to remove the salt, then pat them dry with kitchen paper.

Sweat the onion, chilli, ginger and garlic in the oil in a large saucepan until see through. Add the chopped aubergines, tomato and butter and stir. When the aubergines have softened, add the lemon zest, juice and balsamic vinegar. Add the coriander at the last minute.

When both dishes are nearing completion, cook the pasta until al dente. Combine the 2 sauces and stir through the linguine. You might also like to add basil and olives.

Serve with grated parmesan cheese.

A spin on a classic Italian vegetarian pasta dish.

PORTHMINSTER BEACH BREAD

We make this bread every day at the Café, twice a day in summer.

- 550g strong white bread flour
- 10g sea salt
- 20ml rapeseed oil
- 7g dried yeast (or 10g of fresh yeast)
- 300ml warm water
- Large pinch of caster sugar

Preheat the oven to 200°C.

Pour the warm water into a measuring jug, add the yeast, sugar and oil and stir with a fork. Stir the flour and salt together in a big bowl, make a well in the centre and pour the wet mixture in. Mix everything together roughly before turning out onto a floured board.

Knead the dough for 20 minutes or 10 minutes in an electric mixer. Once you have a smooth and elastic dough, nestle it back into the bowl and cover in cling film, ensuring there are no air gaps. Leave the dough to rest in a warm place for an hour or until it has grown twice in size.

Shape your dough so it fits evenly into a well-oiled large loaf tin, dust the top of your loaf with a bit of flour and then cover the tin and leave in a warm place to double in size again.

Slash the top of your loaf and place on a baking sheet in the preheated oven. Throwing a cupful of water onto the baking sheet will create a steamy environment for the perfect crust.

Cook for about 25 minutes or until golden, the bread is cooked when it makes a hollow sound if you tap it at the bottom. Leave for at least 10 minutes on a cooling rack before slicing.

STICKY ASIAN PORK
with Pickled Cucumber

A really popular dish, using a classic Chinese cooking process. Most meats will braise well in this stock - try duck, quail or beef.

Our master stock is around 4 years old, which gives it a fantastic depth of flavour. However, if you are re-using the stock, make sure your equipment is exceptionally clean and boil the stock sufficiently to kill any bacteria.

Serves 4

- 1.5kg on the bone pork belly
- 500ml Shaoxing wine
- 200ml light soy
- 100ml dark soy
- 200g golden caster sugar
- 1 orange, peel only
- 2 cinnamon sticks
- 2 star anise
- 1 large knob of ginger, roughly chopped
- 5 cloves of garlic, crushed
- 8 cloves

SAUCE
- 250g golden caster sugar
- 350ml light soy
- 2 red chillies
- 2 lemon grass
- 1 bulb of garlic, cut horizontally

TO SERVE
- Pickled cucumber (see glossary)
- Handful roasted unsalted peanuts, crushed

Place all the ingredients for the pork in a large pot, cover and simmer for 30 minutes, skimming the impurities off the top as you go.

Once the meat is cooked, empty the liquid into a clean pot and boil for 5 minutes, or place in a container and cool to re-use next time.

Bring the stock to the boil and simmer for 5 minutes. Place the pork belly in a deep oven tray, pour over the hot stock and cover tightly with silver foil. Cook in the oven for 4-5 hours, or until the bones are loose and coming away from the pork easily.

Remove the meat from the stock and allow to cool slightly before removing the skin and bones from the belly. Place between two trays, place a weight on top and leave in the fridge overnight. Once completely cooled cut the pork into 10cm squares.

For the sauce, roughly cut the chili and lemongrass, add to a pan with soy and sugar, simmer and reduce by a quarter.

In a lightly oiled hot pan, add the pork pieces and cook on all sides until light brown. Pour a small amount of the pork sauce over so that the pork is just covered and cook on a low heat until nice and sticky.

Serve with pickled cucumber and crushed peanuts.

CIDER BRAISED PORK CHEEKS
with Jerusalem Artichoke Purée

We were trying out different variations of our sticky Asian pork and came up with this dish, pairing the pork with Cornish cider. Perfect in autumn.

Serves 4 as a starter,
or 2 as a main course

- 400g pork cheeks, fat removed
  (you can ask your butcher to do this)
- 200ml Cornish cider
- Good quality apple juice, to cover
- ½ apple
- ¼ fennel bulb
- 1 tsp fennel seeds
- 1 tsp coriander seeds
- 1 tsp toasted pinenuts

JERUSALEM ARTICHOKE PURÉE
- 1 shallot, finely chopped
- 1 clove of garlic, finely chopped
- 25g butter
- 150ml cider sauce (see above)
- 10 small Jerusalem artichokes, peeled
  and diced
- 25ml double cream
- A splash of truffle oil
- 1 tsp toasted pinenuts
- Fresh oregano leaves

Add all the ingredients for the pork cheeks to a saucepan, making sure the meat is well covered. Cover with a lid. Place on a very low heat and simmer for approximately 1 hour or until the meat is tender, keeping the lid slightly ajar.

Remove the cheeks from the pan and set aside for later. Strain the liquid through a sieve, return to the pan and reduce until it lightly coats the back of a spoon.

For the purée, melt the butter in a saucepan and sweat the shallot and garlic until soft. Add the Jerusalem artichokes, coat in the butter and add 150ml of the cider sauce. Cook out the liquid until the artichokes are soft and then blitz them to a fine consistency. Add a splash of truffle oil and the cream, stirring well. Season to taste.

Place a small portion of the purée on each plate, top with the pig cheeks (slice if you prefer) and garnish with the toasted pinenuts and oregano leaves.

VENISON
with Celeriac Purée, Raspberries & Bitter Chocolate Sauce

Serves 4

- 400g venison fillet, cut into
  4 steaks
- 2 carrots, peeled
- 1 bunch of green or French beans
- 50g spinach
- A handful of fresh raspberries,
  broken up

VENISON SAUCE
- 380ml red wine
- 750ml beef stock
- 6 peppercorns
- 3 bay leaves
- 1 tbsp balsamic vinegar
- 1 tbsp sugar (not heaped)
- 500ml chicken stock
- 300ml double cream
- 25g bitter dark chocolate
  (minimum 70% cocoa solids)

CELARIAC PURÉE
- 1 small celeriac, peeled and diced
- 125g butter
- ½ peeled apple, diced
- Salt and pepper

*Raspberries and bitter
chocolate are a classic
combination with venison.
We use wild venison
from Dartmoor.*

With the exception of the chocolate and the cream, combine all the sauce ingredients in a large saucepan, bring to the boil and leave to simmer for a good hour. Skim the mixture occasionally to remove the surface. You need to reduce the mixture to around 200ml, which may involve increasing the heat in the later stages.

While the sauce is simmering, you will have time to prepare the other parts of the recipe.

Melt the butter in a saucepan and add the celeriac to it. Cover with milk, bring to the boil and simmer gently until the celeriac is soft. Strain off any excess milk, add the apple and blitz to achieve a smooth consistency. If you feel it necessary, you can add a little milk. Finally season to taste.

Season the venison fillets and cook in a splash of rapeseed oil in a large frying or griddle pan for approximately 6 minutes on each side, then let them rest for 5 minutes. Slice the fillets - they should be evenly pink inside.

To finish the sauce, remove the bay leaves, pour in the double cream and reduce by two thirds. Stir in the chocolate to melt.

Cut the carrots into ribbons and steam just before serving, along with the beans and spinach. Place a serving of the celeriac purée on each plate and arrange the venison on top. Spoon over the venison sauce, sprinkle with broken raspberries and serve with the vegetables.

SWEET

BROWNIES
& Blondies

Makes 16 brownies

- 400g 60% dark chocolate, broken into bits
- 400g unsalted butter, diced
- A good pinch of sea salt
- 6 eggs
- 500g caster sugar
- 200g plain flour
- 100g white chocolate, roughly chopped
- 100g milk chocolate, roughly chopped

Pre-heat the oven to 150°C. Line a brownie tray (35cm long, 25cm wide, 5cm deep) with baking paper.

Bring a pan of water to the boil and turn it down to a simmer. Find a bowl that fits on top of the pan and break the dark chocolate into it (the water should not touch the bottom of the bowl or the chocolate could burn). Add the butter and salt.

Once the chocolate mixture is melted, set aside to cool. Whisk the eggs and sugar in a bowl until light and fluffy, then add the flour gradually until it's all mixed in.

Add the chocolate mixture to the eggs and beat until you have a smooth, even-coloured mixture. Add the chopped white and milk chocolate and stir.

Pour the mixture into the baking tray and bake for around 20 minutes for brownies that are still gooey on the inside. Cool slightly before cutting into 16 squares.

Serve with a good coffee and a sea view.

Makes 16 Blondies

- 350g white chocolate, broken up into small chunks
- 350g unsalted butter, diced
- 500g caster sugar
- 6 eggs
- 280g plain flour
- 150g ground almonds
- 400g white chocolate buttons

Pre-heat the oven to 140°C. Line a brownie tray (35cm long, 25cm wide, 5cm deep) with baking paper.

Put the white chocolate (but not the buttons) and butter into a large heat resistant bowl and place above a saucepan of barely simmering water, making sure the bowl does not touch the water. Leave to melt very slowly and resist the temptation to stir.

Meanwhile, in a large mixing bowl beat the eggs with an electric hand whisk. Add the sugar gradually and continue to whisk until the mixture becomes pale and fluffy.

When the chocolate and butter have fully melted, allow to cool a little before folding into the egg mixture, followed by the flour, ground almonds and white chocolate buttons.

Pour the blondie mix into the baking tray and cook in the oven for 40 minutes. Allow to cool a little before cutting into 16 squares.

This is our own unique recipe for white chocolate brownies, which have proved a massive hit. White chocolate can be temperamental to work with so be careful with the quantities and temperatures.

MUFFINS
Light & Fluffy

We make these muffins every day, often using what's in season: raspberries from the garden, blueberries, vanilla and strawberry, chocolate, banana and walnut...

Makes 9 muffins

– 220g plain flour
– 2 level tsp baking powder
– 125g sugar
– 180ml milk
– 1 large egg
– 180ml vegetable oil
– A handful of berries/chocolate
(or whatever you fancy)

Pre-heat your oven to 190°C. Line a muffin tray with muffin cases and set aside.

Place all the dry ingredients in a bowl, make a well and add all the wet ingredients. Combine until a smooth paste forms, either using a wooden spoon or an electric mixer. If adding anything other than berries, throw this in now.

Place a spoonful of muffin mixture into each muffin case, filling each to just over halfway. If using berries, poke a few berries into each muffin now.

Bake for 20-25 minutes, or until golden on top. Remove from the muffin tin and leave to cool on a cooling rack. Great served warm with some crème fraîche.

Read and Burn © Anthony Frost

PANNACOTTA
with Rhubarb Sorbet
& Polgoon Jelly

Pannacotta is such a great dessert because you can pair it with so many things, from soft fruit like raspberries and blueberries, to cinder toffee or a dark chocolate sauce.

This version is served with a rhubarb sorbet (stewed or baked rhubarb works well too) and a jelly made from Polgoon, a local sparkling champagne-style cider.

Serves 6

- 225g mascarpone
- 500ml sour cream
- 2 tbsp lemon juice
- 6 leaves of gelatine
- 185g sugar
- 500ml double cream
- 1 vanilla pod, scraped
- 25ml water to soak the gelatine

POLGOON JELLY
- 185ml Polgoon cider, or any good quality cider, sparkling rosé or champagne
- 25ml crème de cassis
- 3½ sheets of gelatine
- 38g sugar

RHUBARB SORBET
- 50ml cold water
- 450g rhubarb, trimmed, partly peeled and chopped
- 85g caster sugar, plus extra to taste
- Lemon juice, to taste

PANNACOTTA

Soak the gelatine leaves in cold water until softened. Combine the sour cream, sugar, mascarpone, cream, and vanilla pod and seeds in a saucepan and bring to a simmer. Remove from the heat, take out the vanilla pod and add the lemon juice. Cool slightly and add the gelatine. Stir to dissolve and then strain through a sieve.

Transfer the mixture to 6 individual moulds (95mm in diameter) and chill in the fridge.

POLGOON JELLY

Freeze 6 shot glasses (thicker glass is better, to ensure the glasses don't crack). Warm the gelatine, 75ml of the cider, sugar and crème de cassis. Pour into the shot glasses and add the rest of the cider quickly: bubbles will set inside the jelly. Cover and cool in the fridge until ready to serve.

RHUBARB SORBET

Place the rhubarb, water and sugar in a pan, cover with a lid and bring to the boil. Continue to boil for 2-3 minutes, then remove the lid, reduce the heat to a simmer and simmer for a further 4-5 minutes, or until the rhubarb is tender. Set aside to cool.

Transfer the cooled rhubarb to a food processor and blend to a purée. Transfer the puréed rhubarb to a fine sieve and push it through the sieve with a wooden spoon, collecting the liquid in a bowl.

Once the mixture has cooled completely, add the sugar and lemon juice according to taste. Transfer to an ice cream maker and churn for 15-25 minutes, or until the sorbet is smooth and has set. Store in the freezer until needed.

To serve, dip the sides of the pannacotta moulds into warm water before turning out onto a chilled serving plate. Add a scoop or two of rhubarb sorbet and serve with the polgoon jelly.

CARAMELISED BANANAS
with Cinnamon Meringues & Pistachio Ice Cream

There are many elements to this dessert, but if you're not feeling too ambitious you could serve them in whichever combination you prefer. Definitely one for the sweet-toothed.

Serves 4

- Half a banana per person
- Caster sugar, to cover

CINNAMON MERINGUES
- Makes 8 individual meringues
- 2 large egg whites
- 110g caster sugar
- Cinnamon, to dust

PISTACHIO ICE CREAM
- 250ml milk
- 250ml cream
- 120g sugar
- 6 egg yolks
- 1 cup of unsalted, shelled pistachios

CINDER TOFFEE
- 150ml water
- 25g butter
- 2 tsp malt vinegar
- 1.5 tbsp golden syrup
- 225g sugar
- 2 tsp bicarbonate of soda

Peel the bananas and halve them lengthways. Place cut-side up in a baking tray and sprinkle over an even layer of sugar.

A blowtorch is best to caramelise if you have one, alternatively you can place the bananas under a pre-heated grill (be careful they don't burn).

CINNAMON MERINGUES
Pre- heat the oven to 140°C. Line a baking tray with greaseproof paper.

Place the egg whites in a clean bowl and whisk until they form soft peaks. Slowly add the sugar and continue whisking until you have a stiff, glossy mixture.

Spoon 8 heaped dessert spoons on a baking tray, dust with cinnamon and bake for 30-40 minutes until the meringues are dry. Turn the oven off and leave the meringues to cool and dry out further for a few hours (or overnight) with the door ajar.

PISTACHIO ICE CREAM
Roast the pistachios lightly in a dry frying pan over a low to medium heat, taking care not to let them burn.

Heat the milk and the cream in a pan. Beat the egg yolks and sugar in a heatproof bowl and slowly pour the hot mixture over the yolks and sugar.

Place the bowl over a saucepan of simmering water and cook until the mixture coats the back of a wooden spoon (this may take a little time and patience).

Blitz the pistachios in a food processor and stir into the mixture. Strain through a fine sieve and cool.

Once fully cooled, churn in an ice cream machine until smooth and thick. Transfer to a plastic container and freeze.

CINDER TOFFEE
Grease a large baking tray. You'll also need a thermometer to hand.

In a large pot (big enough to accommodate the rising bubbles) heat the butter, water and vinegar till the butter is melted. Add the sugar and golden syrup and cook till the mixture reaches 154°C (what is known as the 'hard crack' stage).

Now for the fun bit. Remove from the heat, add the bicarbonate of soda - it will bubble up quite a lot - and continue to stir until the bubbles settle.

Pour into the greased tray and allow to cool before breaking into chunks. You can keep it for a quite a while in an airtight container – if it lasts that long!

PIMMS
Deconstructed

*We came up with the idea of breaking
down the elements of Pimms to make
a dessert, and thanks to Sally, our
pastry chef, this is the result.*

Serves 6

WILD MINT ICE CREAM
- 250ml milk
- 250ml double cream
- 120g sugar
- 10 sprigs of assorted mint in a muslin bag
- 6 egg yolks

STRAWBERRY SHERBET
- 50g icing sugar
- ¼ tsp bicarbonate of soda
- ½ tsp citric acid
- 25g dehydrated strawberries

CANDIED ORANGE PEEL
- 2 large oranges, 0.5 cm cut off top and bottom
- 3 cups of sugar, and ½ cup to toss cooked peel
- 3 cups of water

APPLE AND CUCUMBER SORBET
- 3 Granny Smith apples, cored and chopped
- ¼ medium cucumber, chopped
- 50g caster sugar
- 210ml water
- 150ml liquid glucose
- 1 tbsp lemon juice
- A pinch of citric acid

WILD MINT ICE CREAM

Slowly heat the milk, cream, and mint in a saucepan to simmering point but do not let it boil. Beat the sugar and eggs together in a heat-proof bowl using a balloon whisk. Then, still beating, pour the hot milk mixture slowly over the eggs and sugar.

Return the mixture to the pan and bring it back to the simmer, whisking until the mixture thickens slightly (enough to form a film over the back of a wooden spoon). Again do not let it boil or it will separate.

If you have a sugar thermometer, the temperature should be 82°C.

Pour it into the washed bowl and cool rapidly over ice or iced water. Strain the custard and chill thoroughly in the fridge before churning in an ice cream maker. Transfer to a plastic container and freeze.

STRAWBERRY SHERBET

Blitz the dried strawberries in a food processor or place in a polythene freezer and crush them with a rolling pin. Combine in a bowl with the other ingredients.

CANDIED ORANGE PEEL

Quarter the oranges vertically and remove the peel (not including the pith). Cut into 0.5cm wide strips and cook in boiling water for 15 minutes. Drain, rinse and drain again.

Boil 3 cups of sugar and 3 cups of water in a medium size saucepan over a medium heat, stirring to dissolve the sugar. Add the peel and return to the boil. Reduce the heat and simmer until the peel is very soft, approx 45 minutes. Drain.

Toss the peel in half a cup of sugar spread on a baking tray, separating the strips. Lift the peel from the sugar and transfer to a sheet of foil. Leave until the coating is dry, which will take 1 or 2 days.

Candied orange peel can be wrapped in cling film and frozen for up to 2 months.

APPLE AND CUCUMBER SORBET

Blend all the ingredients in a blender and pass through muslin. Churn immediately in an ice cream maker. Transfer to a plastic container and freeze.

DARK CHOCOLATE BRÛLÉE
with Affogato

*Affogato is a classic that's hard
to beat. Try this version with a
chocolate brûlée - intense, rich
and delicious.*

Serves 6

CHOCOLATE BRÛLÉE
– 6 egg yolks
– 95g caster sugar, plus
  extra for caramelising
– 575ml double cream
– 112g Valrhona or other
  dark chocolate (at least 70%
  cocoa solids)

VANILLA BEAN ICE CREAM
– 250ml milk
– 250ml double cream
– 120g sugar
– 6 egg yolks
– 1 scraped vanilla pod

CHOCOLATE BRÛLÉE
Pre-heat the oven to 140°C.

Combine the sugar and egg yolks in a bowl. Break the chocolate into small pieces. Heat the cream in a small saucepan (don't let it boil), then add the chocolate and stir until it has melted.

Pour the cream and chocolate mixture onto the eggs and stir, but don't create a froth as this will spoil your brûlées. Sieve and pour into 6 ramekins and place in a roasting tin.

Pour enough hot (not boiling) water into the roasting tin so the water is halfway up the sides of the ramekins. Bake in the oven for 35-40 minutes. Cool the brûlées, cover and chill.

Shortly before serving, sprinkle with an even layer of sugar – about 2 tsp for each brûlée. Use a culinary blowtorch to caramelise the sugar evenly.

Serve each brûlée with a scoop of vanilla ice cream and a shot of espresso, to pour over the ice cream at the last minute.

VANILLA BEAN ICE CREAM
Combine the sugar and egg yolks in a bowl. Heat the milk and cream (without boiling) then pour over the egg and sugar mixture. Stir over a saucepan of barely simmering water until the custard has thickened and coats the back of a spoon (it should be 82°C if you have a thermometer).

Cool rapidly by placing over ice, strain through a sieve and chill in the fridge. Churn in an ice-cream machine for 15-20 minutes until frozen.

GLOSSARY

GLOSSARY
Dressings & Seasonings

BLACK SPICE MIX

- ½ cup dry whole coriander seeds
- ½ cup nigella seeds
- ¼ cup whole cardamom pods
- ½ cup Szechuan pepper
- 2 tsp dried chilli
- ¼ cup black sesame seeds

Dry-roast the spices in a frying pan over a low heat until crisp and fragrant. Grind in a pestle and mortar or spice grinder and then pass through a fine sieve. Store in an airtight jar.

PONZU

- 200ml light soy sauce
- 150ml rice wine vinegar
- Juice of a lemon
- 25g bonito (dried tuna flakes)
- 1 sheet konbu (dried kelp)

Whisk all the ingredients together and leave to stand before serving, ideally at least 24 hours.

CITRUS MISO

- 1 lemon, juiced
- 3 limes, zested and juiced
- ½ cup sake
- ½ cup palm sugar
- 3 tbsp white miso
- 2 fresh kaffir lime leaves

Bring the palm sugar, sake and kaffir lime leaves to a soft boil in a pan. Add the miso paste, citrus juices and lime zest and whisk until a sauce forms. Remove the kaffir lime leaves before serving.

THAI SALAD DRESSING

- Juice of a lemon
- Juice of a lime
- 25ml fish sauce
- ½ tbsp palm sugar

Whisk all ingredients together or shake in a jar.

NAM JIM

- ¼ cup water
- ¼ cup fish sauce
- 1 ½ cups rice wine vinegar
- 2 tbsp palm sugar
- 8 red chillies, finely sliced
- 1 tbsp dried long chilli
- 6 cloves garlic, finely sliced
- 2 tbsp grated ginger
- Chopped coriander leaves, to serve

Place the water, fish sauce, vinegar and palm sugar in a saucepan and heat until the sugar has dissolved. Cool and then stir in the other ingredients. Add coriander to serve.

Remove the seeds from the chillies if you don't like your nam jim too hot.

CAESAR DRESSING

- 500ml mayonnaise
- 5 anchovies, finely chopped
- 75g grated parmesan
- 1 clove of crushed garlic

Mix all the ingredients together in a bowl.

GLOSSARY
Stocks

FISH STOCK

- 2kg cleaned good quality fish bones
- 1 medium peeled onion
- 1-2 stalks of celery
- 1 leek
- ½ tbsp white peppercorns
- 2 bay leaves
- 375ml white wine
- 4 litres of water

Clean the fish bones thoroughly, removing all blood, guts, gills and heads.

Chop the celery, onion and leeks into a fairly small dice. Place the fish bones in a large pot and cover with the water and white wine. Bring to a simmer, skimming off all fat as it rises to the surface.

Add the chopped vegetables to the pot along with the bay leaves and white peppercorns. Lightly simmer for around 45 minutes. Let it settle and cool slightly and then strain through a sieve lined with muslin.

VEGETABLE NAGE

- 2 tbsp olive oil
- 4 shallots, coarsely chopped
- 4 small carrots, coarsely chopped
- 1 stick celery
- 2 cloves garlic, chopped
- 1 bay leaf
- 1 sprig thyme
- 1 tbsp white peppercorns
- 300ml water
- 200ml white wine
- Salt and pepper
- 1 lemon, zest only

In a large heavy-based saucepan, heat the olive oil and cook the vegetables, herbs, spices and lemon zest over a gentle heat for 15-20 minutes, until the vegetables have softened but not coloured at all.

Add the water and wine and season with salt and freshly ground black pepper. Simmer for a further 15 minutes.

Remove from the heat and pass through a fine sieve. Use straight away or refrigerate or freeze until required.

CHICKEN STOCK

- 2kg chicken carcasses
- 2 large peeled carrots
- 3 sticks of celery
- 2 medium peeled onions
- 3 sprigs of thyme
- 1 tsp black peppercorns
- 2 bay leaves

Wash the chicken carcasses and remove any residual fat. Chop all the vegetables roughly and set aside.

Place the washed bones into a large pan and fill with water. Bring to a simmer, skimming off any fat that rises to the surface. When all fat has been removed, add the vegetables and herbs. Simmer for 5 hours or overnight on a very low heat.

When the stock has cooled, drain through a sieve lined with fine muslin.

You can keep this in the fridge for 3-4 days or in the freezer for a couple of months (if you divide it into smaller amounts you can then simply defrost the amount you need for that recipe).

GLOSSARY
Sauces & Preserves

SALSA VERDE

– 1 hard boiled egg
– ¼ cup parsley leaves
– ¼ cup basil leaves
– ¼ cup mint leaves
– 1 lemon, zested
– 1 tsp capers
– 4 anchovy fillets
– ¼ cup white bread crumbs

Finely chop the herbs, capers and anchovies. Grate the egg then mix it with the herb mixture, lemon zest and breadcrumbs in a bowl. Slowly add enough olive oil until you achieve the right consistency.

ROUILLE

– 2 small peeled potatoes
– 6 cloves of garlic
– ½ tsp cayenne pepper
– Pinch of saffron
– 2 tsp paprika
– 200ml olive oil
– 3 egg yolks
– Juice of 1 lemon
– Salt

Cook the potatoes in a pan with the saffron and garlic cloves. Drain off the excess water when cooked, reserving a couple of tablespoons. Cool.

Transfer the potato and garlic mixture to a bowl along with the remaining cooking water and mash or blend until smooth. Stir in the egg yolks then slowly pour in the oil until you reach the consistency of mayonnaise.

Finally, add the lemon juice and spices and salt to taste.

ROCKET PESTO

– 5 garlic cloves
– 125g raw pine nuts
– 200g washed rocket leaves (stalks removed)
– 10 tbsp grated parmesan
– 375ml extra virgin olive oil
– Salt and pepper

Place the garlic, pine nuts and a pinch of salt in a blender and blitz. Add the rocket leaves and blitz again before slowly pouring in the olive oil. Stir in the parmesan cheese and check for seasoning.

BABA GANOUSH

– 4 medium to small aubergines
– 1 clove of garlic, crushed
– 3 lemons, juiced
– 3 tbsp tahini
– 200g set greek yoghurt
– Rosemary and garlic, for grilling
– Salt and pepper

Prick the aubergines with a fork and wrap each one in foil with a few sprigs of rosemary and a couple of garlic cloves.

Grill on a barbecue or directly over a naked flame until the skins are charred and the flesh has softened (it's essential to char the skins properly in order to achieve the dish's distinctive smoky flavour).

Remove the garlic and rosemary, scrape the flesh from the skins and blend with the remaining ingredients.

CHERMOULA

– 1 red pepper, roasted, de-seeded and skinned
– 1 tsp dried coriander
– 1 tsp dried cumin
– 1 tsp paprika
– 1 clove of garlic
– ¼ cup flat-leaf parsley
– ¼ cup coriander
– Extra virgin olive oil
– Pinch of salt

Blend all the ingredients together in a food processor and then add olive oil until you've achieved the desired consistency.

MAYONNAISE

- 2 egg yolks
- 290ml groundnut oil
- 50ml white wine vinegar
- 1 tsp Dijon mustard
- Salt and pepper

Put the egg yolks in a large clean bowl, add the Dijon mustard and a pinch of salt. Mix everything well together with a whisk. Then, holding the groundnut oil in a jug in one hand and a whisk in the other, add a drop of oil to the egg mixture and whisk in. You need to take this part slowly. Each drop needs to be fully worked in before continuing with another drop.

The mixture will begin to thicken and go very stiff and lumpy. When it gets to this stage you can add the white wine vinegar.

Now the fragile stage is over, you can then begin pouring the rest of the oil in a very thin but steady stream, whisking all the time. When all the oil has been added, taste and season. If you'd like the mayonnaise to be a bit lighter you can whisk in a tablespoon of warm water.

LEMON MAYONNAISE

Follow the recipe as above, but add just 1 tsp of white wine vinegar along with the juice and zest of half a lemon.

RED PEPPER AIOLI

- 1 red pepper, roasted
- 500ml mayonnaise
- Pinch of chilli powder

Remove the skin and seeds from the roasted pepper and blitz in a food processor, then stir thoroughly into the mayonnaise with a pinch of chilli.

TARTARE SAUCE

- 500ml mayonnaise
- 75g cornichons, finely chopped
- 75g capers, chopped
- ¼ cup chopped flat-leaf parsley
- A good squeeze of lemon juice

Mix all the ingredients together and chill. You can keep this covered in the fridge for 3-4 days.

SWEET CHILLI SAUCE

- 500ml rice wine vinegar
- 600g sugar
- 60g red chillies, diced
- 1 stalk of lemongrass
- Star anise x 3

Place the vinegar and sugar in a clean stainless steel pan and bring to the boil, whisking all the time. Add the finely diced or blended chillies, star anise and lemongrass. Simmer without stirring until it coats the back of a spoon.

PICKLED CUCUMBER

- 1 cucumber
- 250ml rice wine vinegar
- 125g palm sugar
- 2 star anise
- 2 kaffir lime leaves

Peel, halve and de-seed the cucumber and cut into chunky pieces, just under 1cm.

Bring all the remaining ingredients to the boil, then pour over the cucumber whilst still warm. Leave to cool before serving. This will keep in the fridge for up to a week.

TAMARIND AND CHILLI JAM

MAKES 4 JARS
- 1kg fresh tamarind – podded and de-pipped
- 500ml water
- 250g palm sugar
- 100g caster sugar
- 1 tbsp rice wine vinegar
- 1 bunch of coriander, stalks removed
- 3 tender stalks of lemongrass
- 5 shallots
- 50g ginger
- 4 dried chilies
- 5 kaffir lime leaves
- 2 cloves of garlic, peeled
- 1 tbsp sesame oil

Put the prepared tamarind in a large pan along with both sugars, water and the rice wine vinegar and bring to the boil.

Take off the heat, pour into a liquidiser and blend until a smooth paste forms. Pour back into the pot and return to the heat.

Blitz all the other jam ingredients together in a food processor. Fry the mixture off for about 3 minutes over a medium heat and then add to the tamarind paste. Cook for a further 3 minutes.

You can place this in a sterilized airtight jar and keep in the fridge for about a month.

This jam is used as an ingredient in our monkfish curry, but it's also great served with Thai crab cakes, tempura fish or vegetables.

HISTORY

MID 1930s
Café opens and runs for a couple
of seasons before closing at the
start of the Second World War.

POST-WAR
The building is used as a store for
deckchairs and windbreaks, with
the takeaway running downstairs.

1991
The Café is taken over by present
owners and re-opened, proudly
boasting the first espresso
machine in St.Ives.

Sitting almost on the site of where the Café is today, the grandly named 'Pavilion' was built in 1913 to house local concerts and opera performances. Demolished in 1922, locals nicknamed it the 'Tin Tabernacle'.

Fishermen hauling a seine (pilchard) boat up the beach in the early 1900s

Early 1900s: seine (pilchard) boats sitting on what is now the putting green, while early tourists and beach tents line the sand

1920's beachgoers watching a regatta from the town end of the beach

View from St.Ives railway station in the mid 1930s, with the recently built Café appearing in the background
All historical images courtesy of the St.Ives Archive

STAFF
Past & Present

We'd like to thank everyone who has helped make Porthminster Beach Café such a success over the years, including:

Adam Lane Aiden Stevens Aaron Bailey Alan Doyle Alexander Bonar Alison Stevens Amanda Fox Andrea Blunt Andrew Grant Andrew Gibson Andrew Jackson Becky Clarke Ben Day Ben Donaldson Ben Gould Bethany O'Hara Bradley Jacobson Charlotte Ferguson Cameron Jennings Chloe Whitt Colin Hickie Claire Smith Damien Lukac Daniel Cartwright Daniel Fellows David Walker David Underwood David Down David Fox Dean MacKay Deborah Matthews Donald Bassett Donna Lotzof Edward Wilson Edyta Bubic Elliot Fox Emma Bassett Emma Claire Lewis Emma Taylor Emma Valance Fabian Christoph Fleur Sayer Francine O'Hara Gareth Osment Gary Ninnis Georgina Yates Gordon Cox Graham Hart Grant Nethercott Gustav Bessinger Guy Litchfield Hailee Potts Hannah Eckersley Holly Bradley Ian Cambridge Ian Cathcart Isaac Anderson Iona McLeod Jamie Buchman Jason Finnigan Jimmy Woolcock Jenna Woolcock Joan Parker Joan Wells Joanne Miller Joanne Wiggin Jodie Taylor Joel Todd Julia Sharrock Jonathon Sadler John Lane Johnny Crosby Joseph Griffin Joshua Heard Jowan Pryce Julia Knight Jye Snare Karen Prince Kate Cunningham Kate McWilliams Kathy Woolcock Katy Gibbs Kay Prior Kerry Knight Kirrily Priest Kirsty Oxley Kyrie Crocket Lacey Webb Lauren Ringer Lauriann O'Hara Lee Champion Lesley Silver Liz Toole Lorena Diaz Alvarez Lorna Symons Louise Ogden Louise Oquvist Lucinda Bailey Lucy Bligh Lucy Cornes Lucy Mulholland Luka Toffani Luke Horvat Marcin Trykacz Mark Scanlon Matthew Beal Matthew Riedel Matthew Gibb May Burgess Michael Hart Michael Priest Monica Prince Michelle Finnigan Michelle Matich Michael Smith Nadege Hamdad Nancy Meaney Naomi Norwood Narelle Monks Natalie Thomas Neil Clarke Nicola Robey Nicole Frisina Nicolette Lane Ollie Aylmar Paul Evans Paul Symons Peter Hodge Peter Foulkes Philip Wilson Rachel Lorente Raine Hales Rani Hewson Rebecca Bagley Rebecca Symons Renee Knight Richard Knight Richard Painter Richard Shelton Ricki Conn Roger Symons Robert Parkitny Rodney Kerr Robert Michael Rowan Clifford Ruth Jackson Ryan Venning Ryno Ockhuizen Sacha Pryce Sally Mills Sam Oakey Sarah Peters Sarah Smart Sean Scanlon Seanna Cowie Shane Bailey Sheila Symons Simon Morgan Simon Parker Stephanie Wallis Sophie Taylor Sophie Hardy Simon Pellow Stephen Horn Stephen Martindale Steve Williamson Stuart Cartwright Stuart Cobb Tahnee Horvat Tamara Schallhorn Tania Cartwright Tess Walton Thierry Quintard Timna Wild Tim Symons Timothy Ashworth Tom Chapman Tom Pryce Valerie Cox Wayne Shanks Xaber Ramsden Yann Trehin Zahra Sachak